SEX MACHINE
A MAN'S GUIDE TO WHAT
REALLY PLEASES A WOMAN
IN BED

Also by Charlotte Kane:

Good Sex—A Woman's Guide to Losing Inhibition

SEX MACHINE: A MAN'S GUIDE TO WHAT REALLY PLEASES A WOMAN IN BED

BY

CHARLOTTE KANE

NEW TRADITION BOOKS

Sex Machine:
A Man's Guide to What Really Pleases a Woman in Bed
by
Charlotte Kane

New Tradition Books
ISBN 1932420614

Contents

So you want to be a great lover?

So you've finally found your dream girl and you want to rock her world. Or maybe you've been married to her for years but want to learn how to bring a little spice back into the bedroom. Maybe you just want to know more about how to please a woman once you *find* one to please.

You've come to the right place.

The truth is that pleasing a woman doesn't really take that much. Yes, you read that right. It's really not that hard. The trouble is that most people try to do too much. It's almost like they're trying to love her into submission. You have to know what *not* to do as well as what to do. But this is not to say that you can get away with not doing anything. It *does* take some technique and initiative. However, it doesn't have to overwhelm you or make you feel inadequate. More importantly, it doesn't have to intimidate you.

But it's really not that hard. Let me rephrase that. It's not that hard if you are willing to expend the effort. This doesn't mean you have to jump through hoops or stand on your head; it simply means that you have to want to be the best lover you can be. *You have to want to rock her world, so she'll rock yours.*

Some might ask, *why bother knowing all this stuff?* One word: Satisfaction. Not only for you, but for your lover as well. A sexually satisfied woman is a woman who loves the man who's satisfying her. She isn't going anywhere as long as she is getting her needs fulfilled. Also, a sexually satisfied woman will be more willing to try new things with her lover. She'll open up in ways you can't imagine. She will titillate you and drive you crazy. She'll dress up in sexy lingerie and let you rip the clothes—with permission, of course—off of her body.

In effect, she might just turn into a sex kitten.

Learning to be the best lover is not a skill you're born with. It's a skill that has to be learned. It means paying attention to the body you are making love to. It means expanding your mind to allow new ways of doing things to come into play. It means, simply, allowing yourself to have more fun in the bedroom. Just like a good conversationalist knows how to listen as well as how to talk, a good lover knows how to respond to and recognize his partner's needs.

This is what this book is about. It's about how to get your woman to the point where she's having massive orgasms, maybe even multiple orgasms. It's about learning how to do it right so she'll feel safe and secure in your arms. It's about making the woman in your life the happiest she can be. A sexually satisfied woman is a very happy woman, which, in turn, can make you even happier.

Also, this isn't just limited to the bedroom. Pleasing a woman out of the bedroom is just as important as pleasing her inside it. If you don't pay her any attention except when you're making love, then you're probably not making love as often as you'd like. Am I right? This is just one of the topics that we'll discuss. And, no, there isn't going to be any male-bashing so don't worry.

I've kept this book quick and easy. To me, sex shouldn't be that complicated. It's just something two consenting adults are doing together to bring one another pleasure. It's something that I believe has been over-explained and needs to be discussed in a simpler, less complicated manner. That's what this book is all about.

I want you to learn what really turns a woman on and learn how to be the best lover you can be. Being a better lover isn't just about her, it's also about you. The more you give, the more you are sure to get.

YOU—THE EXPERT ON SEX?

Before you go any further, I want to let you in on a little secret you might be unaware of. And this little secret has caused many couples some angst in the bedroom.

And the secret is? She thinks you're an expert on sex. Yes, that's right. She thinks you're a playboy, a know-it all, horny man of the world. It's true. Now, I'm not saying all women feel this way, but many of us do. For some reason, this particular woman believes that a man should just *know* what to do between the sheets. They think you should be able to do it in your sleep. They think that just because you have a penis and some testosterone, you should be able to please them at the drop of the hat.

Why do women feel this way? It's a cultural thing. I believe it's because the media presents men in a way that makes them seem like all of them have "been around". This way of thinking probably occurred over time due to the men's magazines and porn. Also, many women think that all guys do is talk about is sex. They have a mental picture of men in a locker-room or a construction site or a garage or someplace like that, discussing the juicy details of their sexual goings-on. Who hasn't seen a movie or a sitcom where this doesn't happen? Therefore, it gets engrained in our minds that men are experts on sex.

This might also be due to the romance novels some of us read where the male characters sweep the female characters up and give them mind-blowing pleasure without fail. This, of course, is fantasy. But, for many women, when this doesn't happen in reality, sex becomes a disappointment.

While it is probably true to a certain extent that men do think about sex more than women—mainly because men are usually more open to sex than most women—I don't know many men who really discuss technique and the female orgasm with their buddies. But, because of the culture we live in, women have a tendency to think that men will automatically and instinctively know how give them good sex.

They also might think that if you don't totally please them, then there's something wrong with them—i.e. you don't like them very much and are showing it. "If he really liked me, he should know how to kiss me." Or, "If he loved me, he'd know how to bring me to orgasm."

While locker-room talk and romance novels do have their time and place, many women can't get over the idea that it's just talk and fantasy. These things do have a time and a place but should never become someone's reality. When this happens, expectations get raised too high and things can sometimes be disappointing.

No, this shouldn't give you anxiety. You should see this as an opportunity to understand where women get these ideas so that you can help her get over this stuff. At the very least, it might help you to understand why it's sometimes hard to please her and "nothing you do is right".

While it's true that women sometimes live in a fantasy land as far as sex is concerned, it's not up to you to bring her *out* of fantasy land, mind you, but, perhaps to introduce her into a new fantasy land—the world you're about to give her. Once you understand what she's looking for and you can give her a realistic version of it, she might be open to opting for reality more than fantasy, and you can give her that reality.

So, what do you do? You probably know a fair amount about sex, but want to know how to please the woman you're with right now. (As we all know, every woman is different and what pleases one might not please another.) Do you ask her? Well, yes and no. Asking your lover to tell you what she wants is almost like asking her to reassure you. Not something many men want to have to do. But letting her know you're open to pleasing her should abate some of her frustration at not getting what she wants in the bedroom.

What you can do is this: Listen and pay attention. As you're making love, really listen to how she's responding. If she moans as you kiss her deeply, she's into it and most likely loves it. If she stays quiet the whole time, she might be wondering what you're doing—and why. Are her hips raising a little as you begin to stroke her? Is she pressing in closer to you? You will know via her body language if she likes what you're giving. In a nutshell, if she doesn't like something you're doing, stop doing it. If she likes something you're doing, keep doing it. It's really that simple.

And if nothing you're doing is working at all? It's time to hone your bedroom skills and this is what we're going to work on next.

THE SEX MACHINE.

If you are going to become a great lover, one thing you might need to realize is that men, when sex is concerned, need to be more like machines—sex machines. Please don't put any more into this than necessary. It's not a put-down. It's simply the way things are. This isn't to say you have to be robotic or stiff or mechanical in any way. It's to say, that if you can look at sex from a different perspective and know your place in all of it, becoming a great lover becomes a reality. And how do you do this? By becoming a sex machine.

Yes, I know it does sound somewhat robotic and mechanical, but women do need a little time in order to orgasm through intercourse. They need time to get their groove on. And the only way they can really do that is with a skilled lover. And that lover understands to a certain extent that in order to please a woman, he has to be able to hold up under the strain. He needs to be able not to get "lost" in the moment and to last. He needs to be able to stay consistent in what he's doing until she's satisfied. In essence, he needs to not give himself the option of orgasming until his lover does.

Sometimes, I wonder what men do get out of sex. When I look at it from their perspective, it seems like a lot of work.

Of course, I understand it's a biological imperative and that it feels really good. Yet, it doesn't escape me about how much work it is on the man's part to get his woman off.

When I say that you need to more like a machine, this doesn't mean that you have to start looking at yourself as being made of tin or anything. It just means that men really do have their work cut out for them in order to be good lovers. They have to know when to hold back. They have to know when to thrust. They have to know when to be still and allow their lover to grind against them in order to achieve orgasm. Yes, it is a lot of work, but I'd speculate that it's more of a labor of love, to say the least. Just thinking about bringing a woman to orgasm and the moans that escape her lips is enough to make many men rise to the occasion, in more ways than one.

So, in order to become a great lover, you must first begin to understand what being a great lover entails and part of that is feeling a little like a machine.

One way to understanding this is to visualize yourself being a big vibrator with lips and hands that totally and completely pleasure your lover. This may sound absolutely silly, but that's what men are kind of like in this regard. And you might want to know that most women who use vibrators on a regular basis love them like nothing else. So, be her machine, her big vibrator, if you will, and be ready to take your sex life to the next level.

LET'S TALK ABOUT SEX.

"Let's talk."

I know many men who hate these dreaded words. However, you should be aware that in order to have a more fulfilling sex life, talking about it will not only relax you and your lover but it can open up a whole new world of communication.

I know when my husband and I were first married, we didn't talk about sex. In fact, I was too embarrassed to talk about it. Sure, we did it and we liked it a lot but talking about it seemed to put it in this whole other realm. It was as if we talked about it, it would take away some of the mystery and enjoyment.

But it doesn't. Talking about sex with your lover can help you to better understand each others' needs. And, like I mentioned before, it can help you relax more. Opening up this line of communication is, in my opinion, a great way to become more comfortable with sex itself and with your lover.

And the talk doesn't have to be all serious. It can be fun. You can mention the sex you've had and tell her you'd love to have more like that. Or you can suggest doing things you'd like to do such as role-playing. There might be a slight problem if she's inhibited and doesn't want to talk. She might think talking about sex is un-lady-like and might refuse to even recognize the subject. This isn't a rejection of you, of course. She's simply doing what she's been taught and for some women, talking about sex to their men isn't something they look forward to doing. So, the best option here is to take it slow at first and be willing to hold back. Yet, if you try to incorporate it from time to time, it might let her know that you're willing to ask about her needs and see that she's being sexually fulfilled.

Just being willing to talk about sex is a great way to start losing inhibitions and get to better sex that awaits you and your lover. It also helps to build trust. If you let her know you're ready to take your sex life to the next level, she might surprise you.

So how do you broach the subject? Why not try talking a little about sex after you're in bed? Let her know there's no pressure, but you'd like to discuss how you could make it better for both of you. And, also, tell her you are open to suggestions from her. For instance, after you've had sex, you might mention how good it was. You could say, "That was great!" Or you could mention something you liked that she did. Be specific, too, and praise her efforts if she gave you a good blowjob or she kissed you so hard it made you weak in the knees. The point is, whatever it is that she did and you liked, let her know. This is called positive reinforcement and it works well in the bedroom.

Now, if she gives you suggestions, don't take offense. Just realize she's a human being and she has fantasies just like you do. So what if it involves sex with a stranger in an elevator? Talking about fantasy is a gateway to being able to talk about sex in general. But in order to stay in the kitchen, you have to take the heat. And that means being able to understand your lover is a woman who might not have the same views on sex as you do.

Another thing to be aware of is that you might want to keep the conversation as "vanilla" as possible to begin with. Don't start talking about anything crazy right off the bat. You can incorporate "dirtier" talk later on, which we will discuss later in the book.

However, keep in mind that the differences you two have do not have to become a sticking point. They can be celebrated if you're just willing to talk about sex without any sort of judgment. Why not try it and see where it leads? If it so happens to lead to an argument, then that means she might not be ready yet to talk about sex. If this happens, just apologize and understand that things like this can take time. Just be gentle in your approach and see what happens. It's okay not to jump right in. Take your time and do it at your, or rather her, own pace. You might want to write in a journal about it first. I know some men who never voice their sexual fantasies, and, thusly, never really know what they want. It is important that you open up to yourself before you can open up to her. Being aware of what turns you on is very important and keeping it hidden from yourself is never a good idea. When you're ready, you can then approach her.

On the other hand, don't be surprised if she wants to talk about sex before you even mention it. See this as an opportunity to bond sexually. And then, once she begins to talk, sit back and listen and be happy she trusts you enough to open up.

PRECAUTIONS.

While this may seem a bit obvious, it is important that you are aware that there are dangers that come with having sex. So, before we go any farther, understand that having sex does come with risks, such as diseases and pregnancy. You should be are that you should protect yourself by using condoms and other forms of birth control.

Also, by engaging in certain sex acts such as anal sex, risks can increase. The best thing to do is be aware of risks involved and protect yourself accordingly. Again, using condoms with other forms of birth control is always a good bet. Have good sex but don't be negligent—always think before you act and use protection. And, if you have any questions, don't be afraid to ask your doctor or other health professional.

WHAT DO WOMEN REALLY WANT?

To men, trying to figure out what women want is one of the world's biggest mysteries. However, in reality, it's a simple question that always deserves a simple answer. Women want love and, above all else, they want to be wanted. More importantly, they want to be wanted by the man they want.

That's right. A woman wants to feel wanted. She wants to feel like her man only wants her. She wants her man to give her long looks filled with desire. She wants to feel that she's the only woman on earth. While you know realistically this not to be true and that there are actually other women besides her on the planet, you should treat her like this so she feels wanted all the time. This builds trust and can bring more security in the relationship about.

This is why becoming a good lover is so important. A good lover knows this and he acts on it accordingly. That means, he doesn't check out other women when he's out with *his* woman. He doesn't even really talk about other women. Sure, he can mention them in a passing way, but he doesn't go on about their looks or what skirt they wore to the office party. You may not even mean anything about your comment regarding other women, but you better believe that she's probably looking at you and trying to figure our why you're talking so much about other women.

You probably already know that most women are very, very competitive with other women. I read somewhere once that women don't put on make-up and clothes to really attract males, but they do it to outshine the other women, thus making themselves more attractive than the others. Sure, a woman does dress to impress men, too, but that competitive factor is still there, though it may be on a deeply subconscious level. She might not even be aware that she's doing it, either. It's not something she does just to be catty either. It's a biological imperative that has been around for ages. The more you outshine others, the more potential mates you might have. It's simply about mating and getting her genes into the next generation. In order to do that, she has to look better than and be more attractive than her peers. As I've said, it's simply biology.

The reason why women hate for you to talk/look at other women is because they can get really jealous. Women aren't usually brought up the way men are and that means they aren't told how strong they are. We're usually told how weak we are and vulnerable and that we have to "keep safe", which is good, as it helps protect us from dangers, but bad because it can lead to insecurity. Thusly, we get jealous when we think anyone is stomping around our territory, even if she's ten feet away in a restaurant.

Knowing why women get insecure can make you understand your woman better and cut her some slack on this subject. Women are especially vulnerable to jealousy and insecurity when they first get into a heavy-duty relationship. If you know why she gets jealous over what you may think of as nothing, you're less likely to do it, right? And that means, you're already on your way to becoming a better lover.

Also, the other thing women want is a sense of safety. If you treat her right and let her know you're going to take care of her if something happens, then she might just take real good care of you in the bedroom. A strong man who is willing to stick up for their woman is a huge aphrodisiac for women. Of course, this doesn't mean that you go around picking fights to show her your manliness. It just means that if she gets in a pinch, you don't run with your tail between your legs. It means that you stick around and help her, if necessary. Keep in mind that the strong silent male is a movie stereotype for a reason. Women like men who are strong and being strong for her means a lot. It means you'll be there when necessary. That is the sign of a great lover.

It's not that hard to understand what women really want.

To recap:
- Women want to be loved.
- Women want to be wanted.
- Women wanted to be wanted by whom they want.
- Women want to feel safe.

And that's pretty much it.

A QUICK NOTE.

Your attitude and knowledge about sex is where sex starts for you. The more you know, the better you can be at it. The more you're willing to learn, the less inhibited you become. The more open you are to it, the more relaxed you will be. For instance, if you have trouble going from first base to second, focus your attention on that and see how you can improve. Being willing to learn is the first step in becoming a better lover.

Also, keep in mind that sex does not start in the pants. It starts in the brain. How? First off, you will *see* the object of your desire and this kick starts your brain into releasing hormones necessary for sex.

Since visuals do play a greater part in love making than they're given credit for, it should stand to reason that she also starts "feeling it" by first looking at you. And she needs to like what she sees. So, it might be a good idea to take extra care with your appearance and, if you don't already, start working out a little. I know, as a woman, seeing a man who's in shape tells my hormones he's more than ready to party. And that he can go the distance in the bedroom.

You need to know that women really do like men who take good care of themselves. It's your call, but know that looking good and being in shape will only add to her infatuation of you. And if you're already in shape and look good? Well, kudos to you. Your woman is very lucky.

DOES SIZE MATTER?

This has always been a big question: Does it matter what size your penis is? Well, I guess that depends on who you ask.

To me, no, it doesn't matter. I do believe in the old adage: "It's not the size of the boat. It's the motion of the ocean". And, truthfully, I've never heard one woman in real life talking about the size of someone's penis. Sure, I've heard about the "big" ones, or whatever, but I've never heard any complaints about the "smaller" ones. Women complain more about men who don't know how to please them than about whether or not a man has a small penis.

I think all this talk about penis size might come from the fact that most all men talk about women's bra sizes. You care about how big our breasts are, so wouldn't it stand to reason that we'd care about how big your penises are? Actually, no. most women don't give a hoot. If they've got a good man who knows how to move in the bedroom and rock their world, size doesn't matter. Period. As long as you're pleasing her, she'll be happy with you sexually. Contrary to popular belief, women aren't as preoccupied with penises as men are with breasts.

There is no reason at all to feel insecure about the size of your penis. Seriously. I do believe if you're a good lover, it doesn't matter at all. So, why make it an issue? Becoming a great lover entails accepting yourself as you are. Sure, you can improve on yourself by buying new clothes to look good for your lover or working out, but accepting what God gave you will give you more confidence than plastic surgery. It's yours and be happy with it.

Just to let you know, most times, when I've heard someone talk about the "big" ones, they've complained that the guy didn't know how to move or that it wouldn't fit. These guys might think because they've got a bigger penis then they don't have to do anything but show up. But, as you know, showing up isn't going to do the trick. It's not going to get the job done. If all you work with is your penis, then you've got a lot of work to do. Besides, women don't want to suffer physical discomfort when they're having sex and if a penis is too big, she's going to dread to see it coming. I heard one woman say that big penises were nice to look at but she didn't really want one inside of her. I think this should be your rule to go by. (And if you're lucky enough to have a big one, realize that this doesn't give you a free pass on your technique. If you don't know how to use it, you're not going to get much repeat action.)

Keep in mind that the penis doesn't have to be the showstopper. It should be used, of course, in the way nature intended, but it shouldn't be the only thing you bring to the table. So, looking at it like this, you have to know that *size doesn't matter.*

HOW *DO* YOU PLEASE A WOMAN?

A few questions to think about: *How do you please a woman? How do you get a woman to want to have sex with you? How do you seduce her? How do you get her to respond to you? How do you give her the best sex ever?*

Those are some very heavy questions. Even so, they shouldn't cause you any sort of anxiety or dread. Because, let me just tell you, from my experiences, it doesn't take that much to please a woman.

Pleasing a woman is as much about you as it is about her. You have to be willing to go the distance, to learn your way around her body, to do things that she likes and to learn how to pick up on her signals in regards to how she's responding to what you're doing. You also have to learn how to be patient and not be selfish. In effect, it's about taking care of her needs before making sure your needs are met. Men who make love to a woman are doing just that—making love to her. They aren't just in it to get off.

So, what are the signals? First of all, a moan coming from her lips should speak volumes. Secondly, if she's got her legs clamped shut, that should tell you she isn't sufficiently turned on enough to allow you access. Taking time to really understand her body language when you are making love will allow you to please her more. It will enable you to know what she likes and what she doesn't like.

When you're making love, you have to really concentrate on her. Look at her like there is nothing else you want to be doing at that moment. Turn off the TV and play sexy music when it's convenient. Moan—but not like you're eating a steak—as you kiss her and really get into it. Enjoy the sensations you experience from having your bodies come together.

It shouldn't surprise you that women like sex just as much as men. It's true. We want it just as much as you want it. However, we want it with a lover we can trust, someone we care about and, possibly, love. We aren't all fragile little dolls, either. Sometimes, women like to get down and dirty just as much as men do. Sometimes that means we women like to lose control to our lovers.

Sure, women do want control when it comes to certain things in a relationship, but when it comes to sex, a woman usually wants her man to take control. (Unless, of course, she's a dominatrix and that's a whole different story.) She *wants* you to rock her world. To the point: Women sometimes liked to be treated as sex objects in the bedroom. As with anything, this varies from woman to woman. But, generally speaking, many women like to have sex with a man not knowing what he's going to do next. It's called submission and, at a certain level, women do have to give up control to the man during sex. It can be overpowering but also a complete turn-on.

Women like men to take charge. They have to control everything in their lives but in the bedroom, most women want a man who will do things *to* and *for* them. Sure, in everyday life, we want to be the boss, but once you've got our panties off, we want you do whatever you want to us. That is, within reason.

So, keep in mind that being timid in the bedroom is about the worst thing you can do. Women do not like timid men. Of course, you can't be all over her like a wild animal. Do use some restraint. Yet, don't hold back like you're afraid of her and always act confidently, like you know what you're doing.

On the other side of this, one thing that annoys most women is that men think there are only two parts to their bodies: their vaginas and their breasts. Never ignore any part of her body. There are various gateways—i.e. erogenous zones—that often don't get touched but bring out the lust—to her sexuality. We'll go over each and every one of these in detail a little later. Also, don't just hone in on her breasts or vagina. You can concentrate on her other parts and she'll let you know when she's ready to proceed.

Most importantly, ask her what *she* likes. How she likes to be touched and kissed or made love to. Asking her lets her know you care. Of course, you need to ask her this as you begin to make love, when she'd more susceptible to respond without a "What are you talking about?" Otherwise, bringing it up over breakfast might land you with some egg on the face.

Once she knows you care and want to take care of her needs, she's going to open up like a flower. Trust is so important. Build it and you will have a compatible sex partner. The added bonus is that she'll have one, too. This is a huge step into pleasing a woman. Just knowing that you're open to taking care of her needs will allow her to relax and get into sex more.

The thing to remember is that as you build trust with your lover, the more crazy sex you are going to have. Wait for it. Don't ever force anything. Just do a little at a time and then a little more. Let her know you don't have to always have it like that, but you'd like to give it a try—when she's ready. If you play your cards right, she'll be ready in no time.

ATTENTION AND FOCUS.

I felt that this subject needed a separate chapter, though I did briefly mention it in the previous one. And that's because giving your woman all of your attention and totally focusing on her during sex tells her that there's no place you'd rather be. This, to a woman, speaks volumes. It means for that place and time, you are hers and that allows her to totally give herself to you. Which, in turn, leads to some fantastic sex.

Women can be complicated but sex doesn't have to be. If you're willing to take the time to get her juices flowing, then the world can be your oyster. If you're willing to go the distance, you can have sex so hot it will peel the paint off the walls. Think I'm joking? Why not try it and see?

It might be good to know that good sex starts *outside* of the bedroom. The better you treat her outside of the bedroom, the better she'll treat you inside.

Paying attention to your lover isn't just about giving her your all in the bedroom. It also applies out of the bedroom as well, maybe even more. It doesn't hurt to let her know how much you care about her occasionally. This means giving her small tokens of affection from time to time in the form of small gifts. A rose or bouquet of flowers speaks volumes. A nice gift on her birthday lets her know that you love and care about her. Also, if you're married, never—*ever*—forget your anniversary. Make it a point not to. This lets her know you still want her and you are willing to honor the day you wed with something special for her. And, yes, it is about her on your anniversary. Make it about her. She deserves it, right?

Many men take issue over gift-giving. Some say that they shouldn't have to "buy her love". The fact is, you aren't buying her love at all, and certainly not with a bouquet of flowers or a dinner. Rather, you're buying her favor. If you want her to think nice things about you, you have to do nice things *for* her. And by doing nice things for her, she will do nice things for you. It's called reciprocation. No relationship should be so one-sided that only one member of the couple feels appreciated.

As I said before, always totally focus on your woman. When you're making love, make love to her. Don't allow your mind to wonder. Give yourself without hesitation to her. Also, don't just do this when you're having sex, do it out of the bedroom as well. Even if you're just watching TV at night together. You should sometimes turn to her and smile. This lets her know how much you love her makes her feel more secure and more wanted. If she asks why you're smiling at her, either smile again or say something simple but heartfelt like, "It's just you look so pretty sitting there." (You can say something different, of course, and you should know that it should never sound rehearsed. Just say something nice that you sincerely feel about her and you'll be okay.)

Once she knows that you totally want her, she will be more open to experimentation and you can get to all that good, hot sex.

WOMEN AND SEXUAL BAGGAGE.

You might be a guy who's tried everything to get his woman turned on but nothing seems to work. For whatever reason, she's not opening up to you. If this is the case, it might be that you have a woman who might be carrying around sexual baggage.

By this I mean, she's got issues with sex. Not all women who don't like sex have sexual baggage, of course. And this is also not to say that if she has sexual baggage she isn't enjoying sex. She could be. It is to say, if she does have sexual baggage, she's probably not enjoying sex as much as she possibly could.

The issues could have risen from any number of varying circumstances. Sometimes, some women grow up with overbearing mothers who tell them sex is "dirty" and "disgusting". Other women are also taught to be "good girls" and to always "keep their legs closed". These things, while probably said with the intent of protecting the young woman, can have negative effects. The negative effect might be that she doesn't really get into sex. For instance, she might think that if she gets into sex "too much", she's no better than a prostitute. Another issue she might have is that she might have been used by a previous boyfriend and has vowed to never let that happen again. Situations like this could certainly lead to sexual inhibition.

So, whether she's got sexual baggage or not, what does it mean if she's sexually inhibited? It means she's holding herself back because of all the bad stuff she's come to associate with sex. If this is so, then this is a big hurdle you might have to overcome and you overcome it with love, understanding and compassion. You overcome it by being strong and letting her know that you won't judge her if she has an orgasm or gets into sex. And most importantly you overcome it by being extremely patient.

Most men, luckily, don't ever have to deal with having an overload of sexual baggage or issues with sex in general. Some do, of course, but for the most part, men look at sex as something they want to do and are unafraid of. However, many women don't look at it like this. And what is planted inside the mind at childhood will stay with a person until they deal with their issues regarding sex.

The best thing you can do is try to get her to open up and talk to you about it. Ask her why she doesn't really like sex that much. Keep in mind that some women might see this as an insult because they might think they are really crazy, sexual beasts even though they're not. So, tread lightly on this. If she can't give you a reason, it's usually because she feels you might judge her harshly because of it. After all, in today's world, women are supposed to be as open and free about sex as men, right? Well, this isn't always necessarily the case. The sexual revolution may have happened, but it didn't happen everywhere, especially not in small, rural towns or in households that are very religious.

If you can't get her to open up, you could suggest therapy where she can go and talk freely with someone who, she feels, won't judge her.

Keep in mind, that none of us are born being inhibited. It is only after it's been drilled into our heads that something is "wrong" with sex that we begin to believe it.

Also, many women might think that if they get into it "a little too much" they might be seen as sluts. So, they hold back. This too, should be addressed. And, if and when you address it, you have to let her know that you will not think badly of her if she likes sex.

I know most men love women who love sex. It's like you've got something in common. Yet, women who have sexual baggage will have a hard time getting over it simply because it's become part of their identity. No one likes being a prude but, on the other hand, no one wants to be called a slut.

What your lover needs to realize is that no one is going to give her permission to have good sex. She will have to give herself permission to have it. Many women are waiting for the "right time" to open up and get into it when, in fact, the right time is now. Why waste another day going without good sex when it's there for the taking? You just have to help her overcome the enormous guilt she feels if she enjoys sex.

You can help her get over her guilt. As I've said, you do this by being strong for her and making her understand you won't judge her if she gets into it. If you can help her overcome her issues, you might have on your hands a sexually empowered woman, which, you will come to realize, will be a great gift not only to you but to her as well.

So, if you do decide to talk about this with her, bring it up when there's no one else around and you have a few hours to talk about it. She might spill the beans and let you know what's going on. She might think you're crazy and trying to pin a label on her. Whatever the case, just do it with love, tact and sincerity. You should already have some trust built, so just letting her know it's okay to talk about it might be enough.

However, if she does talk, do not judge and do not get mad no matter how freaky the stuff she tells you. Just sit, listen and be ready to understand what's to come. The calmer and more understanding you are, the better it is for you. When it's over, be sure to tell her how much you care for her and how happy you are that she was able to open up to you in such a way.

In the end, the best course of action is to just be patient and not give up. Just keep trying to get her to open up during sex without judging her. This might even work better than even having a sex talk because if she's wanting to really open up sexually, she'll eventually let herself as she becomes more trusting of you, her sex partner. If you're always there for her, this will give her more incentive to be the wild, sexual being she wants to be.

Not only will this make her a better lover, it will make you an even better lover.

PORN.

You're a guy. So, of course, you like porn. Most guys do. However, your woman probably doesn't.

Bringing porn into your sex play can certainly spice things up between the sheets. It can also introduce a person to a whole new world. It can turn a woman on just as much as it does a man. The only problem is, most women have a problem with porn. And that problem usually lies in the fact that some women might see porn as degrading to all women. They think that women in porn are being used and/or seen as objects, as things that are only there for a man's pleasure.

Another reason many women don't like porn is because they might think their man is comparing the women in the video to them. They might see it as competition in some odd, round-about way. There are many various reasons why women don't dig porn but the point of this chapter is to let you know that if you can help your lover get over her hang-ups about porn, you can really add some heat to your sex life.

And how do you do that? Well, you certainly don't go out and buy a dozen or so pornos and just thrust them at her. And it might not be a good idea to ask her if she would like to "watch a little something" with you. The trick here is to slowly introduce her to porn over time and see how she reacts.

You do this by, perhaps, buying a few tasteful erotic coffee-table photo books. There are a lot of these books available and most of them are done with class and style. It's a more arty way to share porn, but it can get the ball rolling. If she responds well to that, why not get some erotica? There are a lot of erotic novels which can spell out sex about as good as any porn, only without the visuals. If she likes these, why not get some soft-porn videos? And after that, there are actual pornos made that are catered more towards women that you could purchase. It's important that you do this stuff as a couple so that she knows that she's as much a part of the process as you. Otherwise, she may just think that you're forcing the stuff on her.

The thing to do is not share your favorite porn, but to find a balance of things that both of you can watch and enjoy.

Keep in mind that the important thing to do is sit down and share these things with her and, if she eventually responds well to a full-blown porno, then there you go. She might be waiting for you to bring it up. She might not have ever thought about it. But if you give it a whirl, with some taste and sensitivity, you might find your lover becomes just as turned on as you do. And that can only lead to hotter sex. Porn really is a great aphrodisiac. Most women just don't know where to begin, or don't even fathom that they should be watching it.

Also, bear in mind that if she doesn't like it and is responding to your efforts in a negative way, back off and apologize. You don't want to offend her or make her think that you're some kind of porn addict. This is part of responding to her needs that we discussed earlier in the book.

Of course, if at any time, she becomes offended at any of this, just stop. I know most men love porn and I, personally, don't have a problem with it. But, like I said, there are many women who have problems with it and never will like it. In this case, don't push it as it is sure to lead to an argument. It isn't worth arguing about, in my opinion.

Something good to know.

One of the most important things I can tell you is this: Don't be afraid to ask your lover what she likes in bed. And, almost importantly, don't get upset if she tells you. While this may seem like a contradiction, I know that there are men out there who will get upset once their lover tells them what she wants. It may make them feel as though she's "been around the block a few times". To some reading this, this will seem almost foolish but to those who know what I'm talking about, they understand completely. Just take my advice and let all your preconceived notions of how a woman is "supposed" to act in the bedroom dissolve. Because if you "think" she should be this way or that way—and that includes being almost virginal—you're not accepting her as the person she truly is. And if you don't accept her, then how can you hope to form a strong sexual bond with her? You can't. So, therefore, getting over this immature assessment that you may have not only opens up space for deeper communication, but it also lets the light shine in so you can truly see her for that wonderful woman she is.

This type of interaction will in turn will allow her to see what a wonderful, accepting man you are. Good communication is key to a good sex life. And with good communication comes trust. If your lover totally trusts you, this will not only allow you to enjoy each other in bed, but out of bed as well. Developing trust and accepting each other for the people you are is one of the best gifts you will ever give each other.

So, when you ask your lover what she would like and she tells you, do it. If she says she wants it "harder" or "softer" then do it. These tiny clues are letting you know how to bring her closer to orgasm. And once she comes, it's your turn, right?

And when should you ask her? Obviously, not as you're sitting down to dinner in a restaurant or any other public place. It should be in the privacy of your own home. Perhaps when you're relaxed at night watching TV or just as you're settling down to bed at night. Another good time is right as you're engaging in sex. Just whisper in her ear, "What would you like tonight?" and see where it takes you.

BODY ISSUES.

There are not many women in today's world who are totally satisfied with their bodies. It may be all the super-skinny models in all the magazines or it may stem from childhood issues, but most of us have trouble believing we're "that" sexy.

It might be a good idea for you to let your lover know you adore her body the way it is. Some women have trouble with sex just because they don't think their bodies' measures up. I know some women won't even get undressed in front of their husbands or boyfriends and they never have sex with the lights on.

This is a tough issue to tackle but it's good for any man to know and understand. Women get so many mixed messages about "how" their bodies are "supposed" to be that it's unbelievable. Most of us are so confused we dread buying a swimsuit more than a root canal. It's sad, but it's true.

Of course, if your lover has issues with her body, it probably doesn't help much when you tell her how much you love and adore her just the way she is. She probably doesn't believe you. Sounds odd, but it's true. You need to realize this is a very sensitive issue for many women and once they get over it, a whole new world opens up for them.

I was the same way. I never understood how I could be seen as sexy and beautiful. My husband would tell me over and over again but his words never sank in. This might be because any time I opened a magazine, I saw tall, thin women with legs up to their chins. I'm petite but far from looking as thin as these women. My legs are very muscular and I have curves. Even though I knew I was "pretty" and all that, I never felt it. It took me years to feel it and mostly what I had to do was stop looking at magazines and comparing myself to every woman on earth.

In time, I learned just to accept myself as I am, curves and muscular legs and all. This took me a long time, but it was time well spent. I believe that if most women would start just accepting that they don't look like the women in magazines who are, mostly, air-brushed, posed and styled to perfection, then they'd have better body images and be better able to accept themselves. This, in turn, can lead to a better sex life.

This is where you can come in. Telling your lover that you love the way she looks is one way to start. However, don't just say "you look great". Give her a specific. If she has sexy legs, tell her. If she has gorgeous eyes, let her know. Be specific in your favorite body part but let he know that you love all of her, every single inch.

And be understanding. This body issue may seem trite and silly to most men, but it is an issue in today's world. We are bombarded with images that are far from being realistic and then we are expected to adhere to these imagines, which is completely ludicrous. However, letting your lover know how much you love and accept her body as is, is one way to help her get over her issues. And most women have issues with some part of their body. (Plastic surgery wouldn't be so popular if this weren't true.)

If she tells you she "hates" this or that body part, sit her down, hold her hand and ask her to tell you why. And then listen and let her know it doesn't matter. Let her know that you love her body and wouldn't change a thing. With this reassurance, it might not be long before she thinks the same thing.

If she still wants to improve on herself, why not let her take a clue from you? If you start getting into shape with diet and exercise, she might just follow your lead. If you begin to improve yourself, she might want to also. I wouldn't suggest you ever tell her she needs to lose weight or wear less make-up or anything like that. This is sure to lead to a major argument. But if you can start to incorporate it into your life and let her see your dedication, it might give her some incentive. There is nothing wrong with wanting to be fit and in shape. Most women don't do it because they feel it's hopeless. However, if you promise to be right there with her, she might be willing to take that first step. And that first step will lead to a fuller, happier life.

Keep in mind that the more a woman loves and accepts her body, the more she will open up in the bedroom. Getting comfortable with one's body is a great way to break inhibition once and for all.

IS SHE IN THE MOOD?

Before you begin to make love to a woman, it might be a good idea to make sure she's in the mood for sex. As you might know, there are many reasons why women aren't in the mood for sex which include PMS, family stress and issues at work. Women today have so many things to do that sometimes it's hard for them to fathom doing one more thing, like having sex. This doesn't mean she doesn't want it or doesn't even feel guilty for not having it more. It simply means that sometimes there's too much to do during the day to get to the sex.

If she's not in the mood, she's not in the mood. There's not much you can do about it, either. Just try to be understanding and give her some space. If you try to force sex on an overworked woman, there's probably going to be hell to pay, so it might not even be worth your trouble.

It really doesn't matter how long you've been together, or if you've just met. Many men mistake the signs and see green-lights where there is actually a big red stop sign. Perhaps it might be due to being a tad over-eager, as most men always want their women to be in the mood and ready to go. Whatever the reason, you might want to check and make sure she's into it before you proceed. If nothing else, this could save you an argument or embarrassment down the road.

So, just to be sure your lover is ready for your lovemaking. And how do you do that? Always wait for the signal from her that leads to sex. It might be an up tilted head, indicating she wants a kiss, or a hand on the knee. It might be that she wants to cuddle on the couch. It might be that she responds favorably when you make a pass. It might be she wears a sexy nightgown to bed or tells you a naughty joke. Sometimes, she might not do anything but give you a look. When this happens, be open to it and approach her and see what happens.

Whatever she does, you'll know when she wants to proceed onto the best part of the night. And when you do, you can use the rest of the information herein to have a really wild night.

And if you don't get the signal? You can give it a try and ask if she'd like a backrub and then go from there. Or you can take control and give her a good, hard kiss. However, if she's not into it—and there are many reasons why she might not be—just back off. She'll let you know eventually. And once she does, you can give her a night to remember.

SEDUCE HER BY USING ROMANCE.

Before you get to the hot, intense sex, it might be a good idea to romance your lover a bit. Adding just a touch of romance from time to time lets her know how much you care. And, hey, it can be fun for you, too.

As I've said, women really like romance novels, so, therefore, it should stand to reason that they like romance as well. I believe one reason these types of novels sell so well is because women don't get near enough romance in their everyday lives. And, yes, you can give it to her. Women love the idea of a man catering to them occasionally. It makes them feel special and wanted, which is the right formula for a night of romance that may be followed by some hot sex.

If you take a little time to do romantic stuff, she will be grateful. She might think you're after something. However, she won't wonder too long once you start seducing her by using romance.

Romance can lead to seduction which in turn can lead to hot sex. You don't really need that much to romance her and the best way to do it is to either take her out for a lovely dinner at a very nice, cozy restaurant or you can cook dinner for her at home. Let's hope she doesn't fall over in shock.

(It goes without saying that if you have kids, see if they can visit grandma on this night or hire a babysitter. If not, you might have to wait until they go to bed.)

Now what do you need for a romantic dinner for two? Not much. All you need is: Candlelight, some good food and a nice bottle of wine. If you can cook, prepare her favorite meal. If you can't cook, then why not get take-out from her favorite restaurant? And, if all else fails, why not have her favorite pizza delivered? You can still serve it on nice plates and have wine with it. And, don't forget to light the candles.

Does this sound like a lot of trouble? It shouldn't because, really, if you look at it, it's not doing that much. If you've been with your lover any length of time, you know she does lots of stuff for you. Doesn't she deserve some special treatment?

Of course, you're not only doing all this stuff just to sleep with her, but to make her feel special. This is what it's all about. So, when she arrives, greet her at the door with a glass of wine and take her coat. Also, be sure to tell her how beautiful she looks. Women love to be complimented.

Now, let her make herself comfortable in the living room while you finish getting dinner ready. When dinner is ready, go get her, and walk her to the table and before she sits, pull her chair out. It's time for you to serve her, even if it's just putting the pizza on her plate. Also, pay attention to her needs and if she needs some more wine, fill her glass.

After dinner, tell her not to worry about the dishes and go into the living room. After you're settled on the couch, ask her if she'd like a backrub. I don't know many women who would turn this down. So, give her a good rub and tell her you like doing it. (There's nothing worse than a man who hates to give backrubs and complains about it as he does it. And please don't ask her to rub yours. This is all about her.)

A big way to score points here would be to buy some exotic oils for the backrub. If her mouth drops open in shock, just smile. You've impressed her. Good for you.

The backrub may or may not lead to sex and, really, it doesn't matter because this night is about what she wants. It's about getting her to relax. It's about you doing something special for her. If she wants sex, all the better. However, if she doesn't, just smile with satisfaction that you took the effort to please her in this way.

Now, every once in a while, repeat this process. Cook dinner or go someplace nice and always have some good wine on hand. Let her get used to this. It's really nice. Doing this not only leads to great sex, but also tells a woman you care enough about her that you'd go to all this trouble. And that, in turn, leads her to care about you more and allows her to grow more comfortable with you. This builds trust and trust is what you want, especially when you want to seduce someone.

As I've said, it's all about taking care of her, which, in turn, leads her to take care of you. A little give and take ain't such a bad thing.

So why do all this? I mean, why go to all the trouble? Well, it's simple. Chivalry has been on the decline for years and it's pretty much gone. If you want your lover to really get into you, treat her like she's something special. Be a gentleman. Women do so much now it's unbelievable and deserve to be treated better. Men who take the time to treat their women well will have the best of both worlds. She will probably want to have hot sex with you more and will look forward to spending time with you as a couple. Doing things like this adds to your life as well as hers. It makes her feel special and you feel like you're doing something right. In the end, you both win. And, really, it's not that much effort when you get down to it. So why not expend the effort and make your lover feel like someone who has someone to take care of her from time to time?

TREAT HER RIGHT.

As mentioned in the previous chapter, doing special things for your lover will not only enhance her world but yours as well. Once you begin to see treating her right makes life so much easier and better, you will also begin to see that it helps her become more interested in sex. One reason why? Because she' not so tired all the time.

One way to set the stage for sex is to always be considerate of your woman. If she's always yelling at you to pick up your socks or help with the dishes, she's going to start becoming angry with you and see you as a lazy and increasingly less attractive. When this happens, she will begin to hold grudges and you won't be having sex as often as you would like. In fact, she'll wonder what she saw in you in the first place.

Most women hold grudges. We keep score like nobody's business. If, however, you help out once in a while, there will be no reason for a grudge and, therefore, fewer reasons to tell you "no" to sex.

It's not hard to do. Just start being more considerate of her. Today's women hold jobs and, in addition to taking care of the kids, still do most of the housework. It's enough to make any of us a bit crazy. Don't just "offer" to do things around the house, just do them before she even notices that they need to be done. Like the laundry, for instance. Also, don't do it thinking that it will lead to more sex. Just do it because you care. If you can get into the habit of helping out, it'll be that much better for you. If you're not sure, ask if there's anything you can help her with.

Keep in mind that household chores are one of the biggest arguments of today's couples and this is true of most couples. Who does "what" and "when" is always a catalyst for an argument. Dividing chores up and helping each other to do them can be a big improvement to any relationship. And, occasionally it's okay to let a few things slide. Your home doesn't have to be impeccable or pass the white-glove test. Getting it tidy and clean is the easiest way to keep it tidy and clean. All you have to do then is to maintain it. If you can afford it, why not hire someone to come in a do a spring clean? If you can't afford this, take one room at a time and, together, get it clean. Once it's clean, it won't be as hard to keep clean. And that means more time to spend together, as a couple and a lot less arguing.

Another thing, if you have children, why not take them out one Saturday and let her rest for the entire day? As I've said, women do more these days then they ever have and rarely have a spare moment to themselves. Give her time to relax and you might just get some hot sex in return.

And, lastly, why not show her how much you appreciate all she does? One way my husband does this is to bring me a small gift home at the end of the week. Some weeks it's just my favorite candy bar and sometimes it's a rose. It doesn't have to be much, but giving her a little something tells her you do think of her and that you love her enough to do something about it.

It doesn't take a genius to figure out that a man who treats his woman right is a happy man. Isn't doing a little housework or picking up the occasional gift a lot easier to deal with than a constantly pissed-off wife? I think so. In face, I know so.

The gist of it is: You've got to give to get. And, sometimes, giving is better than receiving.

A WORD ON IMPOTENCE.

Sometimes it happens. Please, please don't beat yourself up over it. Most of the time it doesn't mean that there's something wrong with you. Take your time to enjoy what you're doing and you shouldn't even have a problem. I know that you guys sometimes have a hard time with this sort of thing and that's usually because you get so anxious and excited that you psyche yourselves out. Or you can just be too exhausted or too stressed from your daily life. Unfortunately, this can cause more stress and the problem just escalates. So, when or if it occurs, don't start stressing and let things get out of hand. Just relax and don't think too hard. Thinking too hard and trying too hard is a little too much for your penis. It does get performance anxiety.

So take a breath every once in a while and don't worry so much. All you have to do is breathe in deeply and concentrate on her. If you do that, you ain't gonna have a problem.

On the other side of this, your lover might have some issues with your impotence. Yes, yes, I know it has nothing to do *with her*. You know that. Everyone knows that *but her*. Sometimes her feelings might get a little hurt if you "can't get it up". It might sound silly to you, but she can take it personally. No, she doesn't need to take it personally, and we both know it's more of a mechanical issue than anything. However, some women will take it as a personal insult. They might think you don't desire them or want them sexually. The root of this is a low self-esteem issue. It can be overcome, though.

If this happens, just sit her down and tell her it has nothing to do with her. Make her understand this. Make her understand that you're nervous and excited and want to please her so badly that it's causing you problems. Be sure that she realizes that it's not because you're not attracted to her. That's what many women believe when impotence happens. You may know that impotence occurs because of performance anxiety or stress of some sort. Tell her these things and she should begin to understand. Once she does, why not tell her a few things she could do it help? If you like a certain hand stroke, show her how to do it. If you'd like a blowjob in order to help out, ask her for one.

One last note: If you have consistent trouble getting an erection, it's a good idea to see your doctor. While most impotence is performance anxiety related, there is a possibility that it might have a physical cause, so it never hurts to get it checked out.

JACKRABBIT?

A little too quick on the draw, some might say. The sex is so hot and so good, it becomes too much and before you know it—one, two, three, finished! Just like a jackrabbit. Yes, like impotence, this also happens to even the best men at times. They get too excited and the next thing you know, they've ejaculated, leaving their woman feeling a little.... Well, left out.

If this happens to you occasionally, don't worry. However, if it happens on a regular basis, then it might be a good idea to do something about it. Coming too quickly can become a source of consternation for both parties. But it doesn't have to interfere with your sex life if you can get it under control.

As you know, in order for most women to get off during intercourse, they need a little time to do so. That means you have to hold back from ejaculating until she comes.

The biggest thing to do is practice and that means masturbating. As you are masturbating, bring yourself up to the point of ejaculation, then back off. By doing this, it will help you strengthen the muscles associated with holding back and give you an understanding of how to hold it longer. Do this as often as necessary until you have more control of your ejaculations. Also, by masturbating more often, you are desensitizing yourself a little bit and "letting it out", so that you're not quite so revved up the next time you're with her. Regardless, just be sure not to overdo it. You don't want to become an addict or anything.

After you've practiced and are ready to give it a try, then all you have to do when having sex is to put your mind on something else which means, you have to take yourself away from the moment at hand. Also, you have to relax with it. What some men do is think about baseball statistics. Others think of silly cartoon characters. The point is to somewhat separate yourself from it by thinking about something that in no way turns you on. This doesn't mean you can't still kiss her or touch her as she's using your body like a big vibrator. And that's what you are during this time. You're her big vibrator, giving her intense pleasure. What could be better than that? I can't think of much.

GOING TO THE EDGE OF HER COMFORT ZONE.

As you begin to become more of a sex machine, the trick is to push the envelope, but that doesn't necessarily mean you have to go all the way over the edge. This means, if you're interested in getting kinkier in the bedroom, you might want to take it slowly at first before you go all out. Going to the edge of your comfort zone should be enough. Also, knowing when you're going over and pulling back can make sex more exciting for both of you. And that's what it's all about, going to edge and seeing what's there. You don't always have to jump over.

By this I mean, most people have certain standard fantasies. Some of them might include BDSM, spanking or role playing. However, when you and your lover do not share the same fantasies, this is when problems can occur. If you have fantasies of tying her up and she doesn't care much for the idea, you may have a little trouble convincing her. The idea is to try to incorporate these things into your sex life without making yourself or her unduly uncomfortable or making yourself seem like a pervert in the process.

For example, and this is an extreme example, if you think you might be into BDSM or whatever, you can bring some leather into the bedroom, but maybe leave the whips and chains at the door. If you'd like her to dress up like a school girl, then first discuss it with her before buying the outfit. You could say something about how, when you were a kid, you always thought the girls' school outfits were sexy or something. Then, just see how she responds.

Get what I'm saying?

Sex can be a new and exciting world for both of you once you allow walls to be let down. Yet, you have to maintain a delicate balance, such as not pushing for something when you know she's not into it.

Almost all men want a threesome with their lover and another girl. But this isn't something that happens in everyday life. Many—or even most—women aren't that into it for whatever reason. So, you can strike a balance by perhaps reading erotic novels about it or seeing erotic movies which include this sort of play. She doesn't have to go for it, but if she can relax and know it's your fantasy, she can allow you your fantasy. Maybe you can even talk about it during love making. This doesn't mean you have to talk her into it or that she has to do it. It just means that you're keeping it within the safe realm of fantasy. Actually doing it might be too much for her to take, but pretending may be another story entirely.

Also, it's a good idea not to keep going on about your fantasies, especially if she doesn't share them. If this happens, she might start to think you're a creep. Just be casual and never act too hung up on them. Keep in mind that sex is a *shared* intimacy and if one isn't going for something, it won't work.

The point is to be aware of what you want and be willing to push the envelope a little. It doesn't mean to totally overhaul your love life. It just entails tweaking it a little and by going to the edge every once in a while, you can enhance it so much more. As long as everyone is comfortable and a willing participant, there shouldn't be a problem. The only problem occurs when someone pushes someone else into doing something they don't want to. So, in order to avoid this, just don't push. You can suggest, or briefly mention it. However, if you're turned down or she shows no interest, so what? You tried.

KISS HER LIKE YOU MEAN IT.

Kissing is one of the best things a man and a woman share. It's intimate and electric and just feels so good. However, a bad kisser can be a real turn-off. A bad kiss is sloppy and just...*ick.* That's what it is. It's *ick.*

There's no way to tell if you're a bad kisser or not. You may be a great kisser for all I know. However, I want to let you in on some tips that will help you to give her a kiss that will make her weak in the knees.

The best way to be good kisser is to not slobber all over her and to just take it as it comes, moment by moment, step by step. By being relaxed and feeling in control, you can be one of the best kissers out there. In order to do this, just do what feels good and let it come naturally. It's a game of mutual reciprocation. You kiss her and she kisses you. It's that simple. Once you start, you won't want to stop. Also, never force a kiss. If she turns her head away, then stop. However, if she doesn't pull back, go for it. That's what kissing is all about—going for it with complete and total abandon.

Kissing is really not that hard. All you have to do is look her in the eyes. Next, run your fingers into her hair and pull her to you. Keep your hand on her head like you don't want her to get away. And kiss her. First give her a few pecks, and lick her lips. Once your mouths begin to open, put your tongue in hers and just let nature take its course. Don't be all tongue, though. Never all tongue! By this I mean, don't slobber or lick at her mouth like a lollipop. Also, don't force your tongue into her mouth. Just relax and use your lips and tongue gently but with some added force. Let your hands play in her hair. Give her all the sensational delights she craves.

Another way to do this is to just pull her to you and press your lips against hers. Once you feel her respond favorably, open your mouth and just suck at her lips and tongue. Nibble at her lips, press your body close to hers and listen for that moan that is sure to come out of her lips at any time.

In order to be a great kisser, the best advice I can give you is this: Use a relaxed tongue. That's right. Don't use a stiff, pointy tongue. It really doesn't do that much for anyone. And, as you're kissing her, kiss her like you mean it. By this I mean, kiss her like she's the only woman in the world you want to be kissing. And if you're putting this much effort into it, she is the only woman in the world you want to kiss. Probably.

It should be mentioned that you should always make sure your breath is fresh. Either brush your teeth beforehand and use mouthwash or chew a piece of gum. Bad breath is a big turn-off, as you well know, so be mindful of this.

One final note on kissing: Don't reserve these types of kissing just for sex. Kiss her occasionally on the spur of the moment and give her one of these breath-taking kisses and watch her swoon.

WORSHIPPING HER BODY.

As mentioned before, women, these days especially, are very insecure about their bodies. Most of us don't look like models and most of us have a few flaws here and there. Regardless, we want to know that you like, if not love, the way our bodies look and we *don't* want to be compared to supermodels. This is very important to us. We want you to look at us like there are no other women on earth. Really, we do. This gives us power and confidence. This also leads to mind blowing sex.

One of the most important things you can do, as a man who's about to get lucky, is to worship her body a little before you have sex. Let her know you find her attractive but at the same time, don't gush about it. Tell her she looks wonderful and compliment her. Whisper in her ear, "That dress you have on makes me hard for you. You look so hot in it." (Keep in mind that these things shouldn't be said on a first date or anything. You should only say things like this after you've built trust with her and became intimate. Otherwise, she might get offended and you won't have another date with her.) Yeah, that will make her feel *really* special. But leave it at that. Don't gush. Just give the compliment and go on about your business.

Remember to explore her body with your hands. Don't grope her; just run your hands along her body and listen as she moans. Touch her everywhere through her clothes until she gives you the signal she wants more. A signal here would be her moving in closer to you by pressing herself up against your body. Take your time as you undress her. If she wants to help, gently push her hands away. As you pull her clothes off, give her skin some light kissing.

When you have her completely undressed, take a moment to drink her in with your eyes. Isn't she beautiful? Yes, she is. Tell her so. Tell her, "You are absolutely beautiful." This should bring a smile to her lips and a blush to her cheeks.

What you're going to do now is take a little time with each part of her body. You're not just going to jump to her breasts. You're going to take time to get all of her body aroused and ready for you.

Begin by sliding your hands up and down her body. Caress all of her body and don't linger anywhere. Move along at an even, slow pace but not so slow that you ignore her other body parts. (As mentioned before, this is just a guide and does not have to be taken literally. By interjecting your own style into lovemaking, you will become a better lover.)

Concentrate on the most sensuous parts of her body, which include...

- *Her stomach:* Run your hands lightly across it, then lean down and kiss it gently—no sucking action needed here. Just a light hand touch and then move up to...
- *Her chest:* This is *not* referring to her breasts. This is the area above her breasts which doesn't usually get much attention. This is a highly erotic area for

many women and I know that when my man pays attention to this area by running his hands along it and kissing it, I go weak in the knees. Once she's responded by moaning a little, move onto...

- *Her breasts:* Run your hands under her breasts, like you're scooping them up. Lean down and press your face into them, breathing her smell in. Now give them a little squeeze, running your thumb over the nipple until it's hard. As she's responding to this, lean in and lick her nipple, just lick it a little before you pull it into your mouth and suck on it. As you're sucking, begin to pay attention to...

- *Her legs:* Run your hands up and down her legs, then between her thighs, but don't go near her vagina yet. This is very titillating for her. This is going to make her want you to put your hand there soon. But not just yet. Just use a little force and alternate that with a light touch from your fingers from time to time. If you like, you can kiss...

- *Her feet:* Many men don't like the foot thing and if it's not your thing, just give them some attention and a good rub and then turn her over onto...

- *Her back:* Kiss your way down her back and then back up, using a slight sucking motion with your mouth. Rub her back gently as you do, then run your hands over...

- *Her buttocks:* Run your hands up and down them, squeeze them and, maybe, give them a light slap. If you want to get a little dirtier, you can run your hand between her buttocks. A little nibble or two on her buttocks is always nice too. Now you can move on to...

- *The backs of her legs:* Run your tongue all the way down the backs of her legs and then back up. Do this a few times and then gently turn her on her back and begin to kiss your way all the way up her body until you come back to her lips. Now give her a good, hard and passionate kiss. As you kiss her, take your hands and put it between her legs sideways, and encourage her to grind against it. As you do this, pay attention to her...

- *Ears:* Don't ram your tongue in. Just gently stroke her a little around her ear lobes and maybe nibble in it and continue to feel her vagina with your hand. She might be near orgasm now and if she is, begin to kiss...

- *Her neck:* Using an open mouth, clamp onto her neck and give a slight sucking motion, running your tongue along it as you do so. If she's not near orgasm, climb on top of her and push her legs open with yours. Now take both of your hands and put them on either side of her...

- *Face:* With both hands on her face, gently stroke it with your thumbs and hold it as you begin to move in sync with her.

The next part is entirely up to you. Have fun with it. And the great thing about it is that the more you make love to your lover, the more comfortable you become. When this happens, there will be more opportunities for improvisation.

THE CLITORIS—MAN'S GREATEST MYSTERY?

The clitoris is to the woman what a penis is to a man. The clitoris is also a woman's gateway to orgasm and sexual pleasure. If overlooked, it can be almost impossible for a woman to reach orgasm. And that's just a shame.

It's very odd to me that we have all kinds of euphemisms for the penis, but none for the clitoris. Or, none I've ever heard of. But that's unimportant. What's important is that you don't overlook this small wonder. But to some men, the clitoris is a complete mystery. *Where is it? What does it look like? And how do I make it work?*

It's all very easy to understand. However, if you're confused about what it's for and how to use it, take a few notes here. The clitoris is located at the top of the vulva of a woman's vagina. It is a small, round, sensitive organ which usually reacts well to light rubbing and/or a vibrator. The lips of the vagina may have to be parted to examine it more thoroughly. You can also run your finger between the lips until you feel it.

The good news is that there really isn't much mystery to the clitoris. It's there and ready for use, just like a penis. And it doesn't take much to make it happy. You might also like to know that some women actually experience female ejaculation via the clitoris.

In the end, though, it's what you do with the clitoris that counts. I hope that the following chapters can enlighten you.

GOING DOWN.

Going down, i.e. cunnilingus is a great way to please a woman. However, knowing how to do it right is crucial. And why is it so important? Because performing cunnilingus is going to help her open up to you. If she knows you love going down there and pleasing her, she's going to want it more and more. You've been warned.

If you find that your lover isn't open to cunnilingus, it might be because she, herself, has a problem with her vagina. Not a physical problem, but she might think that its "smelly" or disgusting. The vagina is a very sensitive area and many women feel that opening up to a man in that way is exposing too much of themselves. This doesn't mean she's ashamed of herself or whatever. It just means she hasn't become comfortable enough with her sexuality to allow someone to go down on her and give her this type of sexual pleasure.

The point is, to let her know that you don't think of her vagina as smelly or disgusting. You should thoroughly enjoy—if not love—going down on her. If you, yourself, don't like to do it, then she will instinctively know how you feel. And if both of you don't get a big kick out of it, then why bother?

Let's assume for arguments sake that you love to do it and she loves for you to do it. Even if she doesn't necessarily like it—or pretends she doesn't—if you apply these techniques, she might just change her mind and soon be begging for it.

First of all, be sure to touch all of her body and don't just jump in by putting your hands down her pants. Take it slow and then—*slowly*—move your hands down until they are resting between her legs. Slide your hand between her legs and move it backwards and forwards, almost in a rocking motion.

As she's getting more and more turned on, push her back until she's lying down and slide her pants/skirt/whatever off and get between her legs. Begin to nibble at her panties, still taking time to finger/explore her as you're doing this. She should be wet by now and ready for more.

Spread her legs open but don't just dive in. remember, you're not in a hurry. Take your time so that you give her your full attention.

What you are going to do is explore her vagina with your face and tongue. Just like you did with your fingers. Be sure to taste it and kiss it and lick it. Take your time to tease her while you're doing it, pull back from time to time to kiss her lips or her breasts. Then dive right back in as if there's nothing on this earth you'd rather be doing. Love what you're doing and live to do it. Going for it with full gusto lets her know that you don't think its "stinky" or "weird." And that's what she needs to know.

As you are going down on her, try to always use a relaxed tongue. Never a stiff, pointy tongue! And never a tongue flick! Forget what you've seen in porn movies—the tongue flick move is just wrong. That does nothing but make her wonder what the hell you're doing. Lick her as you would an ice cream cone.

If you're ready to give her an orgasm, the next step is really so simple you'll wonder why you haven't been doing it all the time. Ready? Here it is: Give her some sucking on her clit. Not too much as you don't want to hurt her, but just a good, soft suck and don't forget to lick occasionally while you're sucking.

That's right. Pressure. She needs it like you need it to get off, but probably not as hard. Be careful and be gently and, be warned, she might get a little noisy.

Stick your face in there and clamp your mouth onto her clit and then suck gently. The tongue shouldn't be hard, but firm and pliable.

It shouldn't be long until she is bucking up from the bed and getting ready to have one helluva orgasm. She will grab onto your head and grind herself onto your face. All you can do now is hang on for the ride.

If you like, you can do the 69, which is a personal favorite of mine. Everyone gets something out of it. Just have her lie down on the bed and climb on top of her or lie beside her with your penis near her mouth. Now, go down on her and just wait. Soon, she'll be going down on you, too. Or, if you like, she can be on top, which is probably what she'd prefer anyway.

TALK DIRTY TO ME, BABY.

Dirty talk is something many couples incorporate into their love making from time to time. If you want to try it yourself, it might be a good idea to be sure you have a woman who's receptive to this sort of thing. A good way to tell? If she curses regularly in her normal life. On the other side of this, you could also be with a woman who never curses but loves the dirty talk, but only in the context of lovemaking. One way to find out? Give it a try.

Keep in mind that talking dirty is okay in the bedroom but elsewhere, not so much. Only try this at home.

Talking dirty to one another while you're having sex can heat things up. It really, really can. But it has to be done right. When done right, it's husky and passionate and friendly and flirty.

The key is to go easy at first and see if she bites. Of course, you're going to be nervous and don't be surprised if you put your foot in your mouth the first few times. If you do, just laugh it off. Sex doesn't always have to be so serious and it's good to keep it light and airy from time to time.

Go easy for the first little bit. As you're making love, lick her ear and then whisper, "You are so sexy right now."

She should respond with a moan. Or she could yell, "What are you talking about?" If she yells, you probably don't have a chance in having your dirty talk being reciprocated. No big deal. Just let it go.

However, if she responds well, you're on your way.

So say something like, "I love the way you feel right now. I love being inside of you."

If she's into it at this point, it's time to crank it up.

Now start licking her neck and then whisper, "I love doing this to you."

"Ummm…" she responds.

"Tell me what I can do to turn you on more."

Listen and then do it. More than likely it's not going to be anything you can't handle. If she doesn't respond, just go back to doing what you were doing and maybe try again at a later date.

If, however, she does respond, then do what she requested. After you do it, get a little more graphic and say something like, "You're so wet and tight. I love doing this to you." If she's into it, she'll most likely talk dirty back to you.

You're getting the hang of it now. And as you're doing it, ask her to tell you how it feels. Ask her to verbalize it, which will then allow you to verbalize how you feel, with the naughtiest words possible. Interjecting "dirty" words of your choice can be a great way to spice things up, but be selective and see how she responds. You don't want her going cold in the middle of sex.

The idea is to go the edge—of your comfort zone. You don't have to jump over, just tip-toe a little bit. If you don't feel comfortable doing something, then by all means, don't do it.

You don't have to talk dirty all the way through sex. You can eventually just let the sex take over and speak for itself.

SHE'S BEEN A BAD GIRL...

And she needs to be spanked. Spanking someone—or getting spanked yourself—can be nice and fun. But does it mean there's something wrong with you if you want to spank your girl? Probably not.

Spanking does make some women weak in the knees. "Come here, young lady, you're in big trouble!"

And that's all it takes.

Some people think people who do this sort of kinky stuff are freaky. Who are they to judge? It's not hurting anyone, at least not in a bad way. Not much anyway.

There is an art to spanking and if you want to try it, it might be a little awkward to tell you woman you want to give it a whirl. One way to approach it is when you're having sex doggie style. All you have to do is integrate a few slaps to the ass. See how she responds. Most women feel naughty and dirty and oh, so sexual when they get spanked while having sex. She might want more and because she wants more, she gets punished for wanting it, by giving her a few more slaps.

It's hard to say why some women like to get spanked. Just accept that some do. Not all, but some. If you've got a lover who likes it, it can really enhance your lovemaking.

So, if your lover is receptive, why not occasionally give her a slap on the ass when you're not having sex? When she asks why you just did that, say, "An ass like that needs a good slapping, that's why." And say it like you mean it. Say it like she has such a great ass, it would be a shame for it not be spanked every once in a while.

Get the idea?

If she really gets into it, give her a surprise some time when she's not expecting it and the time is appropriate. Pull her into your lap, push up her skirt and give her a good spanking. And by a good spanking, I mean, spank her, don't hit her. Never leave a bruise and never, ever let it get abusive! Remember, you're not punishing or hurting her. You're just playfully slapping her on the bottom. This is just a sex game. So, use a flat hand on the buttocks, not on the hip or anywhere else, just on the buttocks. It can make an orgasm intensify. Or, it can excite a person enough to want to get down and dirty.

But what if she doesn't like it? Then she doesn't like it. Many women don't. If this is the case, move on to something else she finds more favorable.

GETTING MORE OF A GOOD THING: BLOWJOBS.

I don't think any man should try to pressure a blowjob out of a woman. It's something that should happen quite naturally and should never be forced. Even if you've been in a long-term relationship, you shouldn't expect a blowjob. However, you can get what you want if you approach it the right way.

You shouldn't try to talk anyone into giving you're a blowjob. However, as I've said before, the better you treat her, the better you might get treated. If you're free and easy with the cunnilingus, she might take it upon herself to be free and easy with the blowjobs.

If you have a very shy girl, you can direct her hand there from time to time during foreplay. But don't even push her head down towards your crotch in hope that she'll discover you have a penis and want to give you a blowjob.

One reason women are so hesitant about giving blowjobs is that they think it's somewhat degrading. It can make some women feel like sluts. It's true. How this came about is anyone's guess, but if you have such a woman, just assure her that you won't think any less of her if she gives you head from time to time. Keep in mind that you shouldn't just come out and say this or you might run the risk of her thinking you're weird. You have to show it by your actions and you can do this by giving her lots of cunnilingus and encouraging words if she caresses your penis with her hand during love making. The point is to warm her up to it before she'll jump right in.

However, if she refuses to do it for whatever reason, then that's her choice. I wouldn't suggest ever coercing a woman into giving a blowjob—what's the fun in that? But, like I said, you can ask her nicely and see how it goes. You can tell her how sexy she is and maybe she'll be willing to give it a try. If she does, you might have to give her some guidance as to what sort of blowjob you like—with or without hand? Also, if she does this, it might be a good idea not to come in her mouth until you find out whether she likes it this way or not. Be considerate that way. You don't want to ruin a good thing when you're just getting started.

And have fun with it.

HOW TO GET HER TO MASTURBATE IN FRONT OF YOU.

For some reason, all men love to see women playing with themselves. Maybe it's because they love to play with themselves a little *too* much. I get it, sure, but most women don't. But you want to see her do it, don't you? I know you do. Well, here goes nothing.

Don't expect her to do it the first time you ask. She won't. But as you're making out, whisper in her ear, "I'd love to see you play with yourself..." *But don't stop what you're doing!* Tell her this occasionally in the first part of foreplay. Just whisper it and go right back to what you were doing. This will put the idea in her head. You might get lucky and she'll pull back from you and go at it. More than likely, though, it's going to take her a while to warm up the idea. If this is something you really want, just mention it every once in a while, off-handedly as you're getting down and dirty. (Don't mention it except when you're getting hot and heavy because she might think you're a bit creepy if you mention it during dinner.)

Do this occasionally—not every time you're getting busy but every other time—and one day, pull back from her and give her a little cunnilingus and really get into it. Take her hand and place it down there and then pull back from her and see what happens. If she removes her hand, take it, place it back where you want it and sit back and see what happens. She might go for it and give you a show and she might not. Either way, you're still getting lucky, so, really do you have anything to complain about?

How to get her to do it doggie style.

Doggie style. You want it but she ain't having it.

If you want to get her up on all fours, don't ask. She's probably gonna turn you down. Just do this when you're getting hot and heavy. How to? Just turn her over, grab her by the middle and pull her up into position. If she protests and says she doesn't like it, ask her to try it for a few minutes and then you can do whatever position she wants.

You can also start out by kissing her neck from behind and working on her. Don't tell her what you're doing. Just do it and let things happen. It's a natural progression and allows her to "let" it happen without actually verbally okaying it. Just keep her back to you and rub her breasts and body as you proceed.

Once you've got her up in position, take your time to keep kissing her back and sucking on her neck. As you make love to her, keep paying close attention to her body. Be sure to put your hand on her clit. Let her rub against it and if you can get her off like this, she'll ask *you* to do it again.

Another good thing to make her enjoy the position even more is to get her vibrator out and place it on her clit. That way she gets double the pleasure. Many women love doggie style after they try it. You just have to get her to give it a shot.

USING VIBRATORS TO ADD PLEASURE FOR THE BOTH OF YOU.

Most women already have a vibrator or two. If they don't, it's my belief they should get one—pronto! (If your lover doesn't have one, why not get her one as a gift?) However, most of them keep them in a drawer and deny their existence, at least around you. You want her to play with one but she doesn't want to let you see. Of course, you will need to be in a relationship for a while to do this—you can't just pull out a vibrator, gift or not, in the early stages of a relationship. Keep in mind that a vibrator is a very personal thing for most women. Also, sometimes she just doesn't want to share everything with you.

However, if you bring the subject up, she might be willing to try. A good way to do this would be to suggest going to an adult bookstore or doing a little adult shopping online together. This is something you can do together and adding sex toys to your bedroom play is a great way not only to get her unbelievably aroused, but to have sex hotter than you can imagine.

The best kind of vibrators are the ones that have a dildo part and little stimulators for the clit area. They move in all kinds of ways and go by the name of either "Beaver" or the "Rabbit". They are unbelievable and every woman should own one. Another good kind is the one called the "muscle massager" and it is just a basic vibrator with a big head that just rests on the outside of the clitoris for intense pleasure.

It might be a good idea to let your lover try out her sex toy by herself without you for a while. Later on, when she's grown comfortable with it, you can ask her about it. And then you can suggest getting it out while you make love. Once you've got your/her vibrator, just have her lie back and use it on herself, if she's willing. If not, ask her if you can try it. If she's game, then be very gentle as you place it on her body. As she's getting off to the vibrator, kissing her breasts or lips can greatly add to the pleasure. She might even have two or three orgasms with a vibrator.

As with anything, bring this subject up with as much delicacy as you can muster. There's no sense in ruffling her feathers over it. If she's willing to bring a few sex toys into the bedroom, all the better. And if not, don't push it. There's no reason why something like this should be cause for an argument. But you don't know until you try. And trying can be part of the fun, especially if she's never used a vibrator before. Just don't be upset if she becomes attached to it. The vibrator should never been seen as the enemy or as if it's getting more than you. It should be seen as a tool that helps a woman open her sexual potential.

One last thing: Many women can't achieve an orgasm without a vibrator. So, if this is the case, don't get insulted. Just be glad she can have fun with her toys.

A MIND-BLOWING POSITION.

Here's a good position for you to try. Start in the doggie position and then both of you lie down on the bed. (Her belly will be on the bed and you will be on top of her.) Spread her legs and ease into her. Now position your arm around until your hand is flat on her clitoris and as you ride her, she will ride your hand. Hold your hand still and tell her to move against it. Keep the kissing up and if you can get to a breast, suck on that. It won't take long for both of you to come.

A GIFT FOR BOTH OF YOU.

There is something your woman can try while you're engaging in intercourse that will not only give her a mind-blowing orgasm, but might help you have one, too.

It's called "The Squeeze". This is something I just happened upon one day when my husband and I were making love. I just found myself grinding against him, then squeezing my vagina around his penis and the next thing I knew, I was having a throw-your-head-back-and-let-the-scream-erupt orgasm.

It was pretty intense, to say the least.

It's not that difficult to achieve but she has to be pretty turned on and wanting it. It might take a few tries to actually do it but keep practicing as it is well worth the wait.

As you are having sex—missionary style, as it doesn't really work that well on top or doggie—you will need to hold still for a minute while you're deep into her. Now she will squeeze her vagina around your penis. (This is kind of like doing a Kegel, which is a bladder strengthening exercise that mimics holding your urine.) Now she will use your penis in the same way as a vibrator. She will clamp onto it and ride it while squeezing her vagina around it. Now she will have to grind against it, and soon, hopefully, she will orgasm.

If done correctly, she might just have a massive orgasmic scream rip out of her throat. That's how powerful this type of orgasm is.

Keep in mind that you might have trouble not climaxing while she's doing this. You will need to hold back and wait, though, until she's done. And once she's done, it's your turn.

So how are you going to tell her about this? While you're making love, just whisper in her ear, "Squeeze it, baby." This means she'll have to squeeze her vagina around your penis. If she doesn't get what you're saying, you might have to talk a little dirtier and say, "Squeeze your pussy around it, baby, like you're trying to squeeze the juice out of me." She should get it then. And if that doesn't work? Let her read this chapter.

COMING ON HER BREASTS.

Men love to come on women's breasts. I know this to be a fact because I've seen a lot of porno movies. It happens all the time in porno, but in real life? It probably happens more than you think.

So you want it but don't exactly know how to get her to let you do it. It shouldn't be that hard. But be warned, you will have to ask first, otherwise, you're going to have a fight on your hands.

This goes without saying, but you probably need to be in a relationship for a little while before this would even be considered. When you've been together for a while—or when you're having sex on a regular basis—you can start slipping it into your sex talk, as you're having sex, that is. When women are turned on, they're more likely to do this sort of stuff.

So, whisper in her ear, "Can I come on your tits?" as you lick her neck. She should respond with a, "Ummm…I guess so…" If she doesn't respond? She doesn't want you to do it. You can ask twice, but three times will probably spoil the mood. Never do it unless she says it's okay! If you do, you will have one pissed off girl.

If she says yes, then do it. After you do it, it's your mess to clean up, okay? Tell her to hold still and go get a washcloth and clean it up as she may not care to clean it herself. Be sensual when you're doing it and say stuff like, "That was so hot that you let me do that," and, "You are the sexiest girl in the world."

And you know what? If she lets you do that kind of stuff, she is. Give her another good kiss. She deserves it.

If you approach it right, she'll interpret it as that you really love her breasts and her body. This is a big turn-on for many women. Most won't don't mind but you have to ask and don't assume that all women will like it. Remember never do anything without her permission. If you do and she takes it as you're taking average of her, you will have broken her trust. And that can be hard to build back up.

ANAL.

Anal sex is much more common now than it used to be. It's not the taboo subject it was years ago. For many people, anal sex isn't something they do all the time. It's usually something that's done occasionally. It's different and a bit naughtier than normal, everyday sex. It is a good way to get off but I've known many people who have tried it once and that was more than enough. If you haven't done it yet and want to give it a try, first of all you are going to have to make sure your lover wants it as much as you. After all, she's the one taking it, if you know what I mean. So, really, it's all up to her. If she doesn't want to do it for whatever reason, let it go. It's not that big of a deal.

First of all, you must introduce the subject. You can't just blurt it out, either. This is going to have to be done during hot and heavy love making. Your lover is going to have to be really turned on to do anal. And by that I mean, she's going to have to be very wet. Also, even though she is already very wet, she is probably going to need some lube as well, so have some handy. One more thing, it's always a good idea to use a condom when you have anal sex. Due to the tearing that can happen, there's a greater chance of catching something. *Always use caution!*

If you find yourself in the throes of passion and wanting to explore a little more, slide your hand between her butt cheeks. See how she responds. If she's into it, explore that part of her for a little while, just sliding your hand up and down and then slip one finger into her anus. Easy does it. Don't jab it in there, just slip it in. it should go in pretty easily.

Now ask her how it feels and if she would like more. You will need to do this in a sexy way, not in a gruff manner. Just ask her, "Baby, does that feel good? Want me to do more?" there's a good chance this might be all the sensation she wants so be prepared to back off. Keep in mind that you shouldn't push this and only go as far as she wants you to go. She'll probably let you know when you're doing more than she can stand. If this happens, back off completely.

If she's responding well and wants to give anal sex a try, try it with your fingers at first and this should get her used to it a bit. Eventually, if she likes it, she'll probably want more. If so, why not get a smaller vibrator and have it around for this occasion? You should be able to tell if she's really into it and, if so, use the vibrator on her—only with her permission, of course.

Once she's ready, you will spread her butt cheeks and the vibrator in very slowly and very carefully. Keep in mind that you can rip the skin *very* easily. This is a very sensitive and delicate area. She is going to feel enormous pressure. If she enjoys this, ask her if she'd like more, i.e. you.

If she gives the green-light, be very, very gentle.

Get behind her and gently ease your penis in. Very slowly. Once you are all the way in, you might not be able to ride her very hard until she gets into it. When she's ready for you to get going, she'll probably start grinding against you. One way to ensure she's getting into it is to lean over and press your hand against her clit. This way, she can come too. (Though some women can come from anal intercourse without help, this is very rare, so she might need help.) If you like, you can put her vibrator against her clit or she can hold it there herself as you're doing this.

And then, let nature take its course. It might take a few tries to get it right. Afterwards, be sure to wash everything and don't go straight into regular sex afterwards until everything is clean. You don't want to get any sort of infection.

Always be safe and be aware of the threat of AIDS. Wear a condom!

A QUICK NOTE ON FOREPLAY.

The important thing to keep in mind about being a good lover is that you don't always have to go through every single motion to get to good sex. Sometimes, your woman might surprise you and want to go straight to the intercourse. I know that I'm not always in the mood for every single part of foreplay. Sometimes, just a little kissing and stroking is enough to get me going. Not all body parts have to be checked off before sex occurs. Sometimes, we women like to get to the intercourse and don't have to have all this foreplay. However, you do need to realize that many women reach orgasm during foreplay and that's why they like it so much. If this is the case with your lover, why not give her what she needs? Sex is about give and take and giving a little before getting is always a good way to go.

The thing to do is take subtle cues from her and go with the flow. If she immediately parts her legs, she's probably ready for the sex. As I've said, women don't always have to have it the same way and usually don't want it the same way every time.

And that's what good sex is about—letting it come naturally without anything being forced. The point is to mix it up and do whatever feels good in that moment. Not all these body parts have to be touched during sex and not all bases covered. Sometimes, it might be more exciting to just go for it and let whatever happens, happen.

Being a good lover is knowing when to take command and also when to hold still. It's about knowing how to read her signals and how to know what she's in the mood for on a particular day. She'll let you know. She's in the driver's seat, remember? You're probably going to get to come regardless of what she wants to do. It's the getting there that's the adventure.

And knowing that while foreplay is always a good idea, some days it's not absolutely necessary. That doesn't mean you have to give it up indefinitely. It just means some days, women like quickies.

ENCOURAGE HER.

Another way to be a great lover to encourage your lover to show her stuff, to let loose and really let go, to really let herself run wild. In the bedroom, that is.

As your sex life gets hotter and intensifies, it seems that the inhibitions you both once had just drop away and you will want to try all the things that you've fantasized about for years. If so, encourage her. Encourage her to dress up in lingerie. Encourage her to leave the lights on. Encourage her to get naked and walk around the house. (That is, if you don't have kids or can send them away to grandma's, of course.)

If she wants to wear a super-slutty outfit, why not do it in the confines of your bedroom? What if she wants to wear it out on the town? Just be sure to go somewhere where this appropriate, like a club. If she wants to go out dancing, take her. Becoming a great lover is also about living a good life full of fun and excitement. This can happen in and out of the bedroom. Take a chance every once in a while and go for what you want. And encourage her to do the same.

This goes without saying, but there are limits to this. If she wants to do something foolish or dangerous, you might want to not encourage her. She might become so comfortable sexually that she might want to go farther than your relationship can handle. Be aware of her and your boundaries. The point isn't to lose your mind, but to lose your inhibitions. And that's a good thing, right?

THIS IS HOW YOU DO IT.

This is what it all comes down to. All of the previous chapters lead up to this. This chapter is just about what to do from start to finish. It's written almost in an erotic novel way and I did that mainly because I find most instruction on matters of making love to be too clinical. With all that said, let's do it.

Start off with a kiss...

Run your fingers into her hair and pull her to you. Keep your hand on her head like you don't want her to get away. And kiss her. First give her a few pecks, and lick her lips. Once your mouths begin to open, put your tongue in hers and allow her to suck on it, and then suck on hers. Don't be all tongue, though. Never all tongue! Use your lips and let your hands play in her hair. Give her all the sensational delights she craves.

Now begin to explore her body...

As you're kissing, begin to run your hands along her body, taking your time to explore. Allow your kisses to linger and then allow your hands to make circles along her back, then down to her buttocks and then down to her legs. Take your time! This is her time for pure enjoyment. Most women love lots of foreplay because that's when most have their orgasms. So, the more, the better. Give her what she wants. Always use a relaxed but not a limp hand to rub her and then use the tips of your fingers as you make your way around her body.

It's time to make her weak in the knees by kissing her neck...

After a little while of this, bend down, move her head to the side and kiss her neck, sucking on it—but not too hard, you don't want to give her a hickey—gently but urgently. Remember, it's not all about T&A. There are erogenous zones all over the place as I've discussed before—her neck, behind her knees, etc. Pay attention to all of these areas and worship each and every one before moving back to her mouth and kissing her more.

Do a bit more body exploration...

And as you're kissing her, bend her back on the bed, settle between her legs and begin to explore her body with your hands. Take your time! Don't just jump to her breasts. As you're doing all this, she should be doing stuff to you. Ahh, doesn't it feel so good? Enjoy the sensations of your bodies moving together. Enjoy the moment, the movements. Enjoy every part of it. Linger, linger, linger on her body, worship it and then tell her how beautiful she is.

Just look her in the eyes and say, "You are so beautiful."

She will melt. As I've said, women are so insecure about their bodies these days it's unbelievable. By letting her know how special she is, she will begin to think you're special too. And you will say it because you believe it. She is a beautiful girl. Just look at her. What a lucky guy you are.

It's time to undress her...and play with her breasts...

Now start undressing her and as you do this, continue to kiss her as you unbutton her top and unsnap her bra. Run your hands across her breasts lightly, and give a gentle squeeze. Squeeze them a little at first, play with the nipples and then run your tongue over one and such it into your mouth. She should most definitely respond favorably to this.

Going down on her is an art form...

It's time to go "down there". Her legs may or may not be clamped shut and if they are, it doesn't necessarily mean she doesn't want you to have access. It might mean that she's getting so much sensation, a bit more might drive her over the edge. Believe me, she wants you to go down there at this point. But go slowly. Follow her cues and don't force yourself between her legs. When she's ready, she will let you know.

Begin by sliding your hands up and down her legs and then by sliding them between them, just a little at first. By playing with her at first, you are letting her know you're not going anywhere without her permission. Those legs should open up soon. And then you begin your exploration into her nether regions.

Now get that skirt/pants off. She should help you do this and once it's off, leave the panties on. Yup, you heard me. Leave them on. (At least for now.)

Take a good look at her vagina. She wants you to look at it, believe me, she does. So take a moment before you dive in and after it's over, lean down, press your face between her legs and breathe in.

This will drive her *crazy!*

Using one finger, slide it under the ridge of her panties, then in. Do this gently and using your thumb, begin to massage it. It is so wet down there, isn't it? If for some unknown reason it's not, it's your job to get down there and *make it wet.* She needs to be wet for easier access.

Now move the panties to the side and begin to lick her. Pull back and slide one finger between lips and then back up and down for a few minutes. Take your time to explore! Women love to be touched down there, not gouged! Don't poke her with your fingers or it'll remind her of her gyno exam. Gently separate the lips and play with her. Caress her clit gently. No rubbing that thing! Don't treat it like a scratch-off! That's a turn-off!

Look up at her and whisper about how much you'd like to put your finger in there. "It's so wet," you say. Now, take your finger and push it into her—gently! If she pushes you away, then move your finger again. If not and she responds well, slide it up and let it explore her for a little bit while you keep your thumb on her clit. By this time, she should be writhing with pleasure. Are you about ready to give her an orgasm? Take those panties off now.

Get between her legs, spread them open and dive in. Going down on her, is a fine, fine art. You are going to explore her now with your face and tongue just like you explored it with your fingers. Go for it. Taste it. Kiss it. Lick it. This is getting her prepared for what you're about to do. Take your time to tease her a little. Pull back after a kiss and then go right back in. And do all of this like there is nothing in the world you'd rather be doing. Treating her right when you're down in her stuff is going to get you some really, really good sex.

Now are you ready to give her that orgasm? Okay. Listen to me. What you are going to do right now sounds so simple you'll wonder why you haven't been doing it before. *You are going to suck her with a gentle intensity.* She needs pressure but not so much that could lead to pain. She needs it as much as you do to get off. She will go through the roof if you do it right. Never use the flick of the tongue on your girl—that does nothing! (I know you've seen this in porn, but remember that stuff is just for show.) Always use the relaxed tongue on her, like you're licking an ice cream cone or a lollipop. Like you're locking on something you really enjoy. Stick your face in there and clamp your mouth onto her—gently, never roughly!—concentrating on her clit and then suck her like there is no tomorrow. The tongue shouldn't be hard, but firm and pliable.

By this time, she is bucking and is probably getting ready to have an enormous orgasm. If she is, you will know. She will grab onto your head, she will grind herself into your face and she will hold you down there until she is spent. Once she's done, it's your turn.

It's your turn...

Climb back on top of her, settling between her legs, and begin to kiss her, allowing her to taste herself. This can be a huge turn on for the both of you. Kiss her like you did before—passionately and with vigor. And ease into her with your penis. She might gasp a little but unless she pushes you away, she's ready for it. Just look at how wet she is now. (If she's not wet at this point, you've got more work to do.)

As you are riding her, she may or may not be able to go for another orgasm. It, again, depends on the woman. Start slow and just enjoy being inside her. Look into her eyes and kiss her, suck on her neck and on her nipples while you gently squeeze the other breast with your hand.

By this time, you should be about to burst. But why not give her a little something for the road? Why not give her another mind blowing orgasm? Do you have it in you? Let's see if you do.

After you've done this for a while, whisper in her ear, "I want you to have another orgasm."

She probably wants another one, too. If so, let her get on top and ride you. As she is riding you, hold tight and don't move! Do not move and let her fuck you. I know it's hard, but do it. She should come pretty quickly and once she does, it's your turn.

Now put her back on her back. And as you're riding her, do it hard. (Be sure she's into it, though.) When you do this, she's still feeling the effects of the orgasm and this will make it intensify. Once you've had your orgasm, hold her tight and linger in the afterglow...

Keep in mind that the main thing is to respond to what she does. Take your cues on how far to go by noticing how she's responding. She will let you know what she wants you to do if you just pay attention. Don't get too wrapped up in the mechanics of it.

Keep in mind, also, that you will have to hold off on ejaculating for a while when you do this. So, practice and start calculating those baseball statistics. And good luck.

BECOMING "THE ONE" AGAIN.

Once we get into "serious" relationships, it's inevitable that we stop becoming a mystery to each other. But it doesn't have to be this way. I say, start it up again, become a mystery like you used to be and fall in love all over again. Putting the spark back into your relationship entails things just like this. It entails giving longing looks and secret smiles shared between the two of you.

Of course, if you are in a new relationship, this might not apply as much. But keep in mind that paying attention to your relationship is very important. You don't have to stop caring or loving. As long as you keep putting something into it, you will get something out of it.

I know that, as a woman, men don't need that much to get going as far as sex is concerned. That's why, in this book, it might seem like it's more about her than you. And that's because it really is, in the end. If you can sexually satisfy a woman, you will always have a place in her heart, even if you break-up or whatever. She'll always look at you as the guy that could get her off. Being a good lover is more about responding to her needs than getting your needs met. The reason for this is simple: Men don't have that many needs to fulfill. I don't mean this in a condescending way, either. I think it's great. Sometimes, I envy men and how freely they can use their bodies in order to gain pleasure. Men, simply don't have as many hang-ups about sex as women. Then again, maybe that's why we, as women, have greater needs.

But it isn't all one-sided. By meeting her needs and paying close attention to her, you are ensuring your needs will be met as well. If you continue to please your woman, she might just continue to please you.

Sex is give and take. It's also a lot of fun, so never, ever keep score. Just do what comes naturally and go with the flow.

And always spend quality time with each other. Do things you enjoy even if it's just walking around the park. This will bring you closer and form a more intimate bond. Which can, as we all know, lead to good sex. The more comfortable you are with each other, the more comfortable you will be in your sex life. It's that simple.

The most important thing you can do for your lover is to tell her how much you want her. And, of course, mean it. As long as she knows you love and want her, she'll be happy. Remember, she wants to be wanted like nothing else. Women do get a sense of power from this.

And let her treat you right from time to time. If she offers a backrub, take it. But don't you be stingy with them, either.

One good piece of advice I can give is this: Don't ever start acting like roommate with each other. Stop yelling about the dishes and the bills and just sit down and talk about these problems as they arise, so they can cease being problems and just things that have to be done. Start supporting each other. It's not that hard to do this and once you start, life will get better.

Once in a while, tell each other what you find special about the other. And do something fun and spontaneous.

Here are a few fun things to do together:
- Go outside at night. Get a blanket and make love (when you're ready) under the stars.
- Go have your pictures taken together. Buy a frame it and put it up with all your other artwork. Do it. Don't wait! Go now!
- Practice hearing each other's fantasies and your reactions.
- Cook in a meal together, just the two of you. Do not order in food of any kind. And, if you have kids, send them to grandma's.

Things to do and for each other:
- Slaps on the ass—it's playful!
- Make a point to ask each other how your day was.
- Listen.
- Turn off the TV while talking or having sex because it's distracting.
- Give each other backrubs.
- Call each other up at work during the middle of the day and ask, "What are you doing?"
- Meet at least once a week for lunch, if possible, or for dinner. *Just the two of you.*
- Take a weekend away together at least once a year.
- Plan a grown-up vacation to Vegas. Stay in a suite and feel like a movie star.
- Buy a good bottle of wine and open it after the kids have gone to bed.
- Move the TV out of the bedroom.

- Do special things for each other like buying a nice, inexpensive gift of Magic Eight Ball or something as silly.
- Get the old CDs out that you used to make love to and listen to them together, recalling those wild times. (Barry White is always a favorite.)
- Do things "just because I love you".
- Never forget why you got together—because you had a spark and fell in love. Remind each other of these things and feel blessed.
- Fall in love all over again and do this by treating each other like lovers instead of roommates.

I say, why not? Let the fun begin—again!

BECOMING A SEX MACHINE AND BEYOND.

Being a good lover doesn't take much. What it does take is a little know-how and some practice. It also takes attention and focus and some sensitivity. These are all things you were born with. You don't have to cultivate anything. All you have to do is bring it up from within you and begin to facilitate it into your sex life.

When we get into relationships long-term, we tend to forget that our lover/partner/spouse still has sexual needs. We get wrapped up in the tedious details of life and work and stress. We begin to overlook special occasions such as birthdays and anniversaries. We forget that our lovers are totally sexual beings and have sexual needs.

You can reawaken yourself and your lover from this haze of the mundane and get back into sex with each other. Or, if you're just embarking on a new relationship, you can start doing things for her that will only make her love you more. And that's doesn't mean buying her diamonds and furs. It means holding the door open for her and helping her with the dishes without being asked. It means giving her a backrub without expecting anything in return and it means being her man when she needs you.

Why not take time and re-familiarize yourself with your lover? Why not make a date? Why not take her out and show her a good time? You can do this and plan it from start to finish. She will be so impressed by this, you won't believe.

When you first started dating, you asked her out, right? So do it again and even show up with flowers and candy. This lets her know that you still think she's a special lady. And you will feel very good about yourself for doing this, maybe even a little smug.

Sex isn't everything in a relationship. What sex does is enhance a relationship and give those two people more intimacy and a place where they can feel comfortable being themselves. A relationship should never been seen as a prison or a harness to keep you back from the world. It should be viewed as a safe-haven, as a place to call home.

However, sex is great and is important, even though we always push it to the backburner when things get crazy. Why not keep it a priority? Sex is really good for your mental well-being as well and releases many good endorphins.

I think we all get hung up on doing it "right". Yet, it doesn't take that much to have a great sex life. Want to know what it takes?

What you need to have a great sex life:
- A willing partner that you trust.
- A place or room in which to do it.
- The ability to listen and respond to each others' needs.

That's all. You don't need lots of money or power. You don't need exotic locales. You just need someone to get down and dirty with. Someone you trust. Someone that you're attracted to. Perhaps, someone you love. All you need is a lover.

You can be a great lover, even a sex machine. Just keep in mind that becoming a great lover does entail trust and love. Without love, sex can be mechanical and that's not much fun, is it?

One thing to remember is to never put pressure on your lover to have sex. Never guilt-trip her so she will have sex just because she feels bad about not having sex with you. If you have to play games to get it, is it really worth it in the end? Begging and pleading are off limits too. If you have to coerce someone into having sex, it won't be much fun for either of you. So, wait until she's ready and then give her the best you've got.

As I said, being a good lover doesn't take that much. But it does take some effort. If you're willing to turn yourself into a sex machine for your lover, the world may just turn into your oyster. At the very least, you might teach her a few new tricks. And then everyone wins.

And that's pretty much what it takes to become a great lover.

Printed in the United States
99447LV00001B/193-213/A